# Canned Goods And Shotguns

## by

# Bill Johnston

Cover Art
originally entitled
"Nuclear Grunge Symbol"
by
Nicolas Raymond
www.freestock.ca
has been altered
(Creative Commons license)

# Contents

# You're Cities Are Burned With Fire

# Isaiah 1:7

*The final transmission from local channel 6 news report: Isaiah Freeman*

"The National Guard is not expected anytime soon."
"I repeat the National Guard is not coming."
"Please stay indoors."
"The rioting has reached its peak now."
"The highways and Interstates are clogged with traffic."
"We have reports that the looters…
(*speaking to off camera*) "Are we still really calling them looters?"
"The looters have long ago picked every store in the area clean and the rioting and fires have gone rampant."
"All communication from the east and west coasts of the United States have gone black."
"I repeat our station has no idea as to the extent of the damage of recent attacks although we do have reports that the damage is cataclysmic."
"I don't know if anyone out there is listening any longer."
"My one piece of advice is to hold your loved one's close."
"Conserve all supplies and water as best you can."
"You are all in my prayers."
"I'm just unsure as to whether or not there is anyone listening."
(*speaking to off camera*) "Then how the hell would you put it?"
(*speaking to off camera*) "Fine!"

"Signing out for the final time from channel 6. This is Isaiah Freeman."

"Welcome to the end."

(*speaking to off camera*) "What? No I won't! Kiss my ass all of you in that fucking booth!"

"Godspeed."

# Therefore Am I Come Baptizing

# With Water

# John 1: 31

I was not born John the Baptist
Burning hells, not even John the Baptist was born John the
Baptist
Let me tell you how I became The Baptist

It began with the moaning
We had the windowless basement and the stockpile
of candles, cans, Culligan bottles, and one book

Eddie had been a hell of a guy
He was big, "big as any man I've ever called friend"
I think I heard a southerner say in a movie once
Hell he knew he was dead
Knew as surely as any man ever has that his time had come
He held that front door against the sill
as we hammered in nails and butted the furniture against it
as no small man of courage or size could have
And when we finished filling the whole hallway
with living room furniture, and the fridge, that door
would surely never be opened on that end
Eddie smiled as he threw chairs onto the pile
and the red ran down his arm
"Keep pressure on it." I told him as he turned to me
His sausage lips parted into a smile and he took a long look
at the gash received at the bite of the axe's head

He said, "Hell, John, the insulin won't keep anyway."
It was just I, Big Eddie, and his two teenage girls
Thirteen and fifteen at the time I think
Though they may never have another chance to celebrate a
birthday

Eddie was clear for a night and a day
We wrapped his arm up sterile as if it mattered
There was no escape
There was no question of wading hip deep in burning chaos to
a pharmacist or a hospital
The cars burned in the streets and we were not among the
hunters in the alleyways, yet
As I said it began with the moaning
We were locked down tight enough that we would draw
no one with the sound, and oh how Eddie moaned
I thought surely he would pass in his first day
I thought he would slip away
Slink into the afterlife on his hands and knees begging for the
lord to let him in the gates
I don't think that anymore
Certainly not the heaven part anyway
They do not call me John the Baptist because I remained
a steadfast, holy man
Eddie moaned for days
The girls held each other for the duration
They shook, only took to several bites of food a day
Accepting the occasional drink of water
Shrinking almost within themselves every time Eddie balled
in his diabetic coma, paused, and then released another
blood curdling scream
They never spoke louder than a whisper into each other's ear
But they stared longingly at me with large couplets of brown
eyes at first in fear and then

one set of them with increasing accusation
In the three days I too ate little. I took to staring
into my large, even then strong hands
Clenching and unclenching them
I read through the bible line by line meticulously
Scribing my thoughts and the stronger points therein
on the yellowing basement walls with care and wet black felt
When I reached the end of the page, and my thoughts
I would tear the page from the book in one straight rip
Right down the spine and roll tobacco in it, light it ablaze
and recite what I remembered of the words I had read
On the morning of the third day
There was not much left of Eddie but still he moaned so loudly
It rang in my head long after he paused to breath in
It still rings in my head
After I filled the bucket and grasped the back of Eddie's head
in my mitt and bent his face into the waiting water
My teeth clenched so tightly I was sure they'd crack and
shatter
My eyes blinked with tears from emotions I wished dead
The fifteen year old said the first words
from either of the two girls
Eddie went limp and the bubbles went from faint to still water
The silence spread like bloodstream into our bodies
"John the Baptist"
Was all she said and all she would say
We did not have enough to make the end of the month
no matter how tight our belts could cinch
John the Baptist would have to tend to his flock

# How Does He Who Sees The Vision See It

## Mary 5:10

We of the Church we always knew
Sure they called us "cultists" and "crazy"
But we bent our backs to the word of God
and the task at hand
We were prepared when rumor came that the first nuke hit
We prayed fervently until dawn that night
As the first light of the sun streamed in
Through stained glass windows and thick steel bars
I had a vision
The Preacher later told me I had begun to shake fervently
That I had risen from a night of kneeling and fasting
And I spoke in tongues only The Preacher
The holiest of our following, could understand
He said that I had told him
Through the language of the heavens
that we would be spared the rapture
Spared to create a new Eden here
among the heathens of Earth
He told the ministry that his word was of the law of God now
and that we must arm ourselves with the fruits of our years of
preparation
To go out into the city and strike down the unbelievers
And that we would reign over mankind as the chosen

# And Of His Fulness Have All We Received,

# And Grace For Grace

# John: 1:16

Abigail and Eva
Those were the girls names by the way
Abigail had a soft heart, long, brown, tangled hair
and an affinity for animals
She had been a vegetarian since the age of 8
and though the family dog was killed
out of sight and quiet, she knew fresh meat when she saw it
She never spoke again after we killed the family dog
She never ate another bite again
Some flowers are not tempered for the fires of hell
Eva on the other hand had always eaten like an animal
Sucking the juice from her fingers after every meal
As her sister Abbie wilted Eva grew from the shit
like a thorned rose
The light in Eva's eyes when any kind of hungry was enough
to strike fear into even me
"She's just meat now." Eva had insisted
when Abigail finally passed
When she said it I swallowed hard
The spit hit long empty stomach
I looked down at Abbie's gaunt, still body
I remember the moment as I pictured Eva and I starved dead
and still beside her
The moment our emotions curdled hard like plaster
The thought of what I must do sent me to shaking fiercely and

gasping for air
Eva merely took me by the shoulders
sat me down in the corner
and went to the kitchen for supplies
Just before her 16th birthday Eva butchered and boiled Abbie
The sound of her at work was horrific
All grunts and the tearing of flesh
I squatted in the corner as she did it
with my face buried in my hands
and when the stew was presented
I had to admit it was the best meal
We buried what was left of Abigail "humanely"
it was not long after that I started bringing home bodies
With Eva as the butcher
To this day I still tell myself it is just pork
it was Eva's idea to decorate the fence
with the corpse's remains
and not 2 weeks pass that we don't add another
head to the fence posts
We have not had a prowler since
After a while one becomes accustomed to the flies

# Not In Bread Alone Doth Man Live

## Jesus 4:4

God why did it have to be a tabby
It's orange fur had bled red around its ankle from the snare
digging into its meat
It was howling so loudly the echoes off the alley walls
were heard from the thing a block and a half away
The bait of a half dead mouse
still kicking slightly in its trap the night before
had drawn the cat right to the snare
I approached the catch
My eyes were locked on the entrance to the alley ahead
for shadows, steps, or movement
I got closer and crawled the last ten feet to the cat
to keep a nearby tire fire from casting my black outline
against the alley wall
The tabby still had some meat on it's bones
I reached it. It hissed and squirmed, thrashing at me
I thrust both of my hands together at its throat
Clenching my hands hard, quieting the thing
Squeezing the life from it as it dug its claws into the arms of
my long sleeved coat and gloves
Though they were leather the dying animal left
rippled furrows in the material and finally went limp
I looked down at it for a moment in the flickering light
I hardly possess the resolve to kill a cat I find familiar
How am I expected to kill the men
that stood between us and salvation
It still wore a collar with the name "Bucky" inscribed on the tag
I had raised six cats in my life before it had become

this struggle
I had always preferred the tabbies
"Bucky," I muttered to myself
"What an odd name for a housecat."
I did not forget to take the rat-bait for soup
I held the dead pet by the tail grimly when I arrived home
I was relieved when its striking similarity
to a former pet went unmentioned
She took it quietly over to the table
with a grim look not seen in her eyes
We rarely spoke but I always saw the relief in her
when I returned unharmed bearing a meal
They say there is more than one way to skin a cat, but she
had mastered just the one.
This had been a joke that drew a grin months before, shortly
after we grew accustomed to eating former pets
"Has it come yet?" I asked
"No not yet, stop asking." she replied
It had been two months
We had to find a way out of the city

# When Ye Come To Appear Before Me

## Isaiah 1:12

*The official transcript of Isaiah Freeman's first day in the Army of Heaven, indoctrination code #00275834, taken as directed in room 23774, building Z33, 21st Century, tier #213*

*Isaiah Freeman:* Yeah... I've been wandering through corridors for hours and...

*Drill Sergeant:* The correct words you are looking for are, "Reporting for duty sir!"

*Isaiah Freeman:* Yeah... about that would you mind if I talked to you for a minute a...

*Drill Sergeant:* You are to refer to me as Drill Sergeant!

*Isaiah Freeman:* Uh... Yes sir. The thing is my mother was Muslim and...

*Drill Sergeant:* We are all servants of God here soldier. Have you not received your induction hallucination and reading material!

*Isaiah Freeman:* Uh yeah, and I'm really grateful to be chosen by God and all...

*Drill Sergeant:* Grateful! You should be down on your knees stroking the Lord's pole for your role as...

*Isaiah Freeman:* Sir none of this is how I'd imagined it.

*Drill Sergeant:* Don't interrupt me slimeball! Now where was I? Have you assimilated your introductory briefing?

*Isaiah Freeman:* Uh, yeah but this reads like cold war propaganda and...

*Drill Sergeant:* Have you manned your post soldier? Report!

*Isaiah Freeman:* Shit I've reported on Jesus, Mary, and twice on John. I'm transcribing everything I sense just like I was told and the thing is…. It all came out as poetry.

*Drill Sergeant:* Well I'll be the judge of that soldier! Charles, Edgar, and William may have a run for their money! Are you a poet warrior soldier?

*Isaiah Freeman:* Sure. I mean, yes sir.

*Drill Sergeant:* Then say it soldier! Are you a poet warrior?

*Isaiah Freeman:* Umm, yes sir. I am a poet warrior, sir.

*Drill Sergeant:* Then get back down there and create! You think God can run this whole pop stand single handedly? Get back in their souls and report back to me when you have something to show for it!

*Isaiah Freeman:* Sir, yes sir!

*Drill Sergeant:* Dismissed!

*Isaiah Freeman:* Just one more thing sir. Why is there a stenographer here?

*Drill Sergeant:* Around here we worship God through Bureaucracy! Every moment of time shall be logged! There is only so much time soldier! Have you ever considered what omnipotence requires of a God soldier!

*Isaiah Freeman:* Well not really. I guess I just thought…

*Drill Sergeant:* We did not pluck you from the valley of death to think soldier! Dismissed!

*Isaiah Freeman:* One last thing. All I can remember of my death is a sharp pain and…

*Drill Sergeant:* Do I have to repeat myself! I said carry on soldier! I have a meeting to make and if I don't beat the cherubs to tee off they'll slow us down all day! Are we understood!

*Isaiah Freeman:* Understood.

*Drill Sergeant:* Understood what?

*Isaiah Freeman:* Sir, understood sir.

# Sister We Know That The Savior Loved You More Than The Rest Of Woman

## Mary 5:5

After him I swore
I would never let another man touch me again
I also swore I would never tell another soul about
the stranger with the dirty floors and gurney
who took every cent I had and left me childless and barren
Scraping out a child and leaving a young woman near death
I begged the licensed doctor that saved my life
not to tell my mother a word
And all he would say when she arrived at the hospital after…
"She'll be fine. She'll be fine."
That night my mother had gotten drunk
and called me a Jesus Freak and a whore
I slept in the halls of our church every night after that night
I refused myself the comfort of a cot in the barracks
I refused myself the sorrow of a woman in mourning
of a nearly grown kid who had made a mistake
I was the first to assembly every morning
Some nights I would pray over the wooden visage of Christ
until the sun cast colored lighting through
our stained glass windows
and I was carried, exhausted, to rest
I have heard the phrase "Mary Magdalene" in hushed tones
everywhere I have gone ever since
I remain the only woman of the community not branded a
"breeder"
And I know now I will never again see my mother

And though I am barren
god has granted me the strength to care for many of his kin
My children are my rifle and my bayonet
I will never again fail God

# Blessed Are The Poor In Spirit

## Jesus 5:3

Settling in,
I open my long leather duster
caked with mud and dark, red, dried blood
The shotgun slips out of its loop clattering to the ground
The inside pocket is turned inside out emptying .22 shells
and red, dirty, 10 gauge plastic tubes
filled with buckshot and primer
And the pistol of six chambers is pulled from my belt
and placed by the latched, steel door
We eat dogfood tonight
The SPAM is saved for a special occasion
The Monty Python skit is called to mind
but we have not had the will for a joke for a fortnight
I shrug the black thick coat free
and catch the smell of myself as I hang the leather on the peg
Cleanliness is next to godliness
And there is no longer any God of concern here
We will hold each other tonight
Excuse without comment the smell of sweat and stench
that rises from our clenched, creviced bodies
We would not forgive ourselves if we took for granted
our last chance to hold one another through the night
She does not ask what the street was like tonight
Bravely hunting stray dogs, crouching still and in prayer when
the shadows of other people grace the alleys of my hunt
We rightly fear one another

Some have taken to our flesh
She does not ask me to kill for us
Perhaps I could if she only requested
Her belly has swollen slowly over time
We do not discuss what the impact of a birth will be
Although our eyes lock in thousands of pages of dialogue
every time she presses a hand to it as she pulls her chair in
At times when the door is latched behind me I curl into a ball
and sob before I make my way into the streets
At times I arrive home and see the streaks
where my wife's sorrow has ran down her face
The snares have been set
Perhaps tomorrow they will bring fat possum
or thin, mangy, scowling cat
We mark the days on a calendar outdated
to clock the months it has been since the now dead radio
promised a National Guard
Every night I hunt slightly farther, one block away at a time
To call this living is open to debate
But I will not allow our passing to occur without smoke rising
from a gun barrel
And without a can of SPAM opened in proper time
in celebration

# For Where The Mind Is There Is The Treasure

## Mary 5:9

I remember arguing that it was Eden
that had given us all everything we hold of value today
"After all isn't knowledge the most important thing we have as
humans?" I had asked in front of the parish
The Preacher had merely clutched his bible until
his knuckles grew white and began to rant of sin
Later The Preacher drew me aside while no one was looking
and hissed that questioning His teachings
would lead me to hell
I never questioned his word again
And when the Preacher called for Holy Warriors to go out
among the beasts of unholy men to scavenge for us
I stood and demanded that I join our men in the hunt
The young men snickered and hissed
some looked hesitant to raise hands
I merely stood as The Preacher shook his head
pulled to eye the rifle they had not been able to remove
from my arms length since the rapture came
and fired true three shots over The Preacher's head
Each round extinguished a lit candle on the wall behind him
He shrank as the shots fired and although I've never voiced it
I briefly wondered why such a man of God feared death
"I am no breeder." I stated fiercely
I was given more ammunition
No member ever questioned my request
to go out on a mission again

It was shortly after that I began to correct others
when they called me "Mary"
I would merely say firmly
"No, not Mary"
"Mary Magdelene."

# For My Flesh Is Meat Indeed

## John 6:55

I had been an animal once
I had served in the military
Thrown my medals made in bloodshed off a bridge
I used to walk to reach my probation officer
After working at day labor
with callused hands and aching back
I had been an animal once
and returning to my "natural state"
It came easier than I had suspected
We faced harder times than those found inside a cell
in a building wrapped in steel in a maximum security prison
When we ate well we exercised hard
Running in place, chin-ups on a jutting door frame
and push ups until those grew to take too long to tire
And then clapping push ups
We carved bows
We shot holes in the drywall across the room
until we could group the arrows we learned to deadly craft well
Soon the gunshots ran rare outside our reinforced windows
You see the factories pumping out cases of gunshot
and the stores that held them
had long ago been looted and empty
And on one of the first days I left the house to scavenge
I brought a man down at thirty yards with my fletching
and when his short, squat companion made a run for it
I ran him down and lifted him from the ground in fury
by the head
He screamed when I lifted him by his skull

and I jammed my thumbs into his eye sockets
Then I slammed him to the ground and strangled the life out of
his useless corpse
I was strong enough to bring both bodies home
dragging them behind me on a length of rope
And when I saw that Eva "The Butcher"
was strong enough to fireman carry them each in for me
hang them from the ceiling by a rope
and gut the two of them to smoke over our flame
I realized that we were two symbiotic beasts
I realized that the world feared us
and not the other way around
I realized I was ready to make trade with The Thumpers

# Thine Anger Is Turned Away, And Thou Comfortedst Me

## Isaiah 12:1

Any interpretation as to how I came upon the words you have read, or will read, will be entirely implausible. Any interpretation of the events described, or to be described, will be equally implausible. I have slipped and skidded through the thoughts of these characters as surely as you are. I am as light passing through their fingertips and soaking Vitamin D into their skin which, if one considers it, is a concept only even considered for an incredibly short period in any timespan of proper perspective.

I am motes of dust in a sandstorm of an improbably vast creation spanning dimensions and therefore the very nature of existence in a way that is inexpressible. It is as one describing pain in words, or, say, an orgasm with letters drawn randomly in a game of Scrabble.

One moment I am the felt tip pressed to the concrete walls of John The Baptist's tormented hands, and in another instance I am a shred of hateful recollection in Mary Magdalene's memory.

I am raw awareness.

One may ask what heaven consists of in appearance and sensation, but I am only aware of visiting once. I am only aware of stumbling through an army base of the envy of any General and an assortment of never ending hallways the envy of any born Bureaucrat.

My very thoughts upon my first visit rang of stenography and in legal script. It was a stark place of stinging florescent lighting and endless, white, drywalled hallways.

I feel myself drawn into the afterlife's embrace. I feel compelled to return with what I have of this variation of three character's perspectives out of thousands of millions of other perspectives of a single of an infinite array of dimensions. My thoughts are free.

This glowing prose. This grasp upon my role. These thoughts that fill me.

Well, as you can see, they are a far cry from my last visit to report back to Heaven.

I am only spirit. Whereas the time before I possessed my customary body and the aching muscles that strained to carry me past endless signs bearing arrows upon walls and plaques upon doors.

In this return I am only soul. I am content. I feel as if I am spiritually swinging low and free in an unseen hammock with every need met.

Several times I have seen the sunrise above the clouds from the cramped view of the window of a Boeing, but embracing me now is the most glorious sunrise and stretch of clouds there has ever existed in any timespan. My eyes would leak tears as I embody this skyline. Though, as I have no eyes, as I am merely perspective, my soul tingles with the pinpricks of an infinite pleasure, and the scenery engulfs me. Is me. Carries me for an infinity.

And then there is someone else to join me.

Though I see nothing.

To me it is a "they".

And as unfathomable as the sensation their presence gives to one with no physical being is. I will refer to them as "Smile".

For a moment I sit awash in their new presence. For a moment I am afloat in bliss. For a moment I am sure I will lie awash in this world for eternity, but I, as so many that have and will live, have grievances.

"Why?" I demand, piercing the contentment of this dimension with stinging question. "Why was my last visit so stark, and why are these three meant to suffer. Why, in fact, am I even meant to record their suffering. This makes no sense."

"The lives of every being that has ever lived consists of seeking purpose. What has led you to believe that your afterlife should be any different?" sang Smile within my perception. "The afterlife shifts with every moment as surely as yours has. You will suffer again as surely as you have before whether through the pain of birth or through embracing the pain of another that has been birthed. This is existence and the questions you ask are an innate aspect of the unending cycle of creation. Keep up the good work Isaiah." Smile lilted.

"Hundreds of millions of lives have been extinguished and I am left to bear witness to the brutality of three! All you have for me is philosophy? All you have for me is a skyline?" I blurted from my inner.

"One cannot light a candle without expecting it to gutter. One cannot light a candle without expecting it to flicker, smoke and one day grow dark." said Smile.

And then I began to slip away from the beauty. Then I began to be pulled at the edges, dragged once again into the desperate inner poetry of desperate people in a dark world that I am uncertain has ever existed in any meaningful way.

Left ringing in my head. Left right up until the point my thoughts were filled with reality I felt the ringing of Smile within my head. I felt them utter, "Smile."

I felt them utter "Smile." And after I slipped within mortal consciousness? I felt hunger.

# Blessed Are They That Suffer Persecution

# For Justice' Sake

# Jesus 5:10

I was lucky
I had been raised in a very bad neighborhood
that the looters had nearly overlooked
And I had been raised with faith
On top of this
For years my mother had dated a survivalist
When she passed away of a slow death of cancer
from inhaling a pack of menthols a day, my father-not-of-blood
had slipped away into the mountains
with nothing
but a pack of supplies strapped to his stubborn back
He swore to never return to our city
Swore with such conviction that he had left me everything
he had struggled to create here
As a younger man, with my mother and I to consider
he had built a sanctuary to survive the end
He had raised me to survive
The house I had inherited had one floor
sunk mostly into the earth, no windows
and was covered in fire-resistant stucco on the outside
I had been raised with a home constructed
with a six inch steel door and frame, double bolted at all times
complete with a steel bar to be lowered under duress
proper ventilation, and a well dug just for our house
We still had a stockpile of candles, flares, matches
camping gear, and not much else

Regret is looking back at the stockpile of imperishable food
you had handed down to you
and had donated to the survivors of Katrina
Regret is a number on an old bank account balance
printed on a piece of paper, that now means nothing
a piece of paper you cannot bear to use to light the woodstove
A piece of paper that up until now meant that
you could one day retire comfortably
Still
He had raised me to survive
Not kill, or help give birth to a child
but I set snares in the night
I tremble when the figures of men draw close
I reach for the double barrel, sawed off shotgun
with a grip that remains unfamiliar
I know I cannot raise a child with a shelf of canned dog food
a mostly empty bag of rice, and a large can of spam
saved for a special occasion
I know the streets are clogged with abandoned cars and killers
I know I am ready to make trade with The Thumpers

# The Excitement Of Death

## Mary 8:19

God has granted me several blessings
Keen eyesight and aim are among them
I was a track star before I dropped out
We took most of the downtown of our city that night
What was left after the fires had guttered out was ours
It was my idea to string the wires
It was my idea to gain high ground
and lure the bikers into our trap
"The Slits" they called themselves
We were well armed
For two years we had been drilling, storing, and praying
when the rapture finally came and left us the Earth
and the sinners to defeat therein
We were prepared
Still
With several of the braver souls of God presenting themselves
as bait
I took a few of the sharper, fitter shots and we split up
Sprinting up countless stairwells to gain high ground
With crowbars and bolt cutters strapped to our backs
It was a turkey shoot
The Slits saw fresh meat and responded predictably
When the wires
Strung at neck height, broke the charge
nearly beheading some
Our men sprung from cover and made God's work of them
With us taking our shots from the lower rooftops
it did not take very long

The remaining cowards left
Throttling away into the night
We crucified the survivors in strategic positions around
our newly claimed territory
And created new strongholds in the buildings
Laying claim to all within
We named the area "Jerusalem"
Although there were some murmurs when
I announced the title
No one would question Mary Magdelene's crack-shot again
I believe it was that night I embraced my greatest sin
I knowingly and with joy embodied true, unrepentant pride
It was not long after that we began to baptize newcomers
after extensive orientation
And we would thereafter be branded among the heathens as
"The Thumpers"

# A Man Can Receive Nothing, Except It Be Given Him From Heaven

## John 3:27

We had been killing for months when the time came to trade
We had behind steel doors, lock and key,
and the all too effective deterrent of severed heads
an impressive complement of goods
My dead diabetic friend
from whom I had gained my namesake and destiny
had owned a garage the size of a small airplane hangar
tucked away behind his modest home.
At the time of his death we had only a half rebuilt motorcycle
and an old muscle car with the engine still in pieces
The value lay in a welder, an impressive collection of tools
and the near lifetime The Butcher had spent
alongside her long ago drowned father
tooling every piece of machinery that had ever seen
the florescent lights hanging from the ceiling of their workshop.
We had acquired a graveyard of motorcycles, countless boxes
of spark plugs, distributor caps, wires, and all manner of parts
we had stripped from every intact car within fifteen blocks
We had weapons, smoked meat, cans of food, vehicles
even medical supplies stashed over a four block radius
The carcasses of past lives had made our larder swell
The Butcher is widely known for throttling her bike into a group
of men, a glistening length of chain in her left hand, and an
engraved, razor sharp hatchet in her right
Ceasing the screams of three or even four at a time

I am not known for hiding in the brush for two days
until something moves and slowly rising to a firing stance
to place an arrow where my gutting knife will go next
I am not known for this because deer and man
do not live to tell
I, The Baptist, am known
for strapping on the bullet proof riot suit
salvaged in a chance shot to the eye of a fool
who should not have removed his helmet
I am known for firing and charging into a crashing wave of
buckshot to hack a man in half with a homemade machete
lifting the shatter proof visor of my riot helmet, and screaming
blood mad red "Run! Run!" as his friends scatter before me
bouncing .22 shells off of my vest, gritting my teeth
to the pain of every bone deep bruise, and cackling,
"One day God will find you, until then run!"


"Say they had anything?" I calmly asked The Butcher
one quiet night after reading the flyer announcing
The Thumpers would soon invoke barter
"Say they had anything. What would you ask for?"
The Butcher looked up at me
from gnawing on a dead man's roasted arm
as I ran my fingertips across countless Bible verses
scrawled on the walls of the basement.
"I don't know." She said brusquely, "What would you ask for?"
"Immunity" I said firmly.
"Well we'd sooner pass the pearly gates of Heaven."
she snorted, tossing the gnawed bone aside.
"I think I'd like to bite into a fresh tomato," I said, "And you?"
I asked and stood squarely before her.
The Butcher stood from a large meal, walked to the pantry
and opened our only can of pineapples chunks
She opened, for what is all intents and purposes

the last can of pineapple on Earth and said
slurping the juice and bits of pulpy flesh from the can
"I want fresh insulin."

# ISAIAH FREEMAN

## presents

# "SAY IT WITH MEANING"

## *The Afterlife With "Drama"*

Dramatized with Isaiah Freeman and "Drama"
Staged and Directed by "Drama"

### CAST
(In the order of their appearance)

Isaiah Freeman, *as*
*himself*...........................................Confused Muse
Drama, *Director*...............................................Angel of
Dramatic Tension

Act I.    An empty stage, lit with a single glaring spotlight,
Afterlife.

### DESCRIPTION OF CHARACTERS

Isaiah Freeman:  A middle aged, paunchy, forlorn figure.
Weary of his time spent in

God's service. Black. Adorned in white robes and pajamas.

Director:   A shadowy figure seated center in the audience in the empty auditorium. His

countenance only lit by the occasional glow of the cigarette in his clenched lips. Grey.

Scene:   *Isaiah Freeman appears from the ether on a large, unadorned stage lit only by*

*an intense spotlight. The seats of the large auditorium are empty besides one. Lit only by the glow of a brightly burning cigarette in a holder is the grey, scaly, barely seen countenance of the director. His clipboard is also in view.*

Isaiah Freeman:   *(center stage, he appears from the ether barely on his feet in the fetal position)*   Cannibalism! Starvation! Slaughter and monotheistic absurdity! Is this what you have placed on my shoulders! Is this what you have brought me into the afterlife to endure? *(springs to standing and moves to front center stage with the spotlight falling behind his movements)*   Just what kind of definition of humanity do you comprehend!

Drama:   *(Inhales deeply on his cigarette briefly lighting a scaly grey facade and a clipboard)*   Okay that was pretty good, but I'm going to need you to stay on script okay? As for the cherub in the rafters running the spotlight. Are you high? I will replace you in a flash. Union or not I own your ass. Okay, Isaiah, from the top. I need you to stay on script for this okay?

Isaiah Freeman: *(Stands front and center stage. A script appears in his right hand. He glances down at it.)* Is this some metaphor for God's plan? Or the need for conflict in our existence? Just what... *(Isaiah glances down at the script seeing every word he's just said written upon it. He begins to fling the script back and forth from his hand attempting to discard it. The script remains stuck fast to his grip.)* You can go to hell! Okay? You can kiss my ass! What kind of ridiculous afterlife would…. You can go to hell! *(glancing down at the script stuck to his hand)* You can go to hell! Shit it says that too. Okay well. Goddamnit! Goddamnit. Goddamnit. Everything I say just appears on this stupid friggin script doesn't it. *(Isaiah holds the script before himself and reads dramatically)* Okay. Thank you for your time almighty prick. I'll show myself out. *(exits from center stage into the ether)*

Drama: Okay! That was good! I can't wait to see what this guy is made of! Cast party here we come! Oh, and as for you fat little cherubs up there? You're a dime a dozen alright. Don't make me tell you again. God I love the theater.

# And When Ye Pray, You Shall Not Be As

# The Hypocrites

## Jesus 6:5

By all that is holy how they did flaunt their ease of existence
The flyer was pasted to nearly every alley wall entrance
I had seen the red cross tags on the walls
I had seen the occasional man crucified
with rickety board to electric pole
They were beyond saving
They moaned so loudly I could spot them from blocks away
They served to be more of a warning
than any string of barbed wire or yellow hazard sign
I had passed the corpses strung up
as Jesus Christ had been
Had I anything in my stomach
it would have emptied onto the asphalt every time
The crows had gotten to their eyes
The sight was as horrific as the backs of my eyelids are
on sleepless nights
One must know better than to blink
After crouching for half an hour
at the entrance of dark silent street
I moved as silently as any man does
having learned to stalk deer as a boy
And when I pulled the flyer from the alley wall
attached to the red scuffed brick with chewed gum
I tucked it into my pocket, checked my snares
with disappointment, stomach gnawing within me
Then slipped home

I pulled the crumpled paper from inside my jacket pocket
after the wife had slipped into bed
She was used to worry holding me awake for days at a time
The thought of what I had seen that day stills the signals in my
mind to freezing
The flyer was simple in it's message
The Thumpers had opened trade
Bring what you could of value to barter
Although that was not what sent me to stutter quietly in
the dark of a single candle
It was that the flyer had clearly been copied in a cheap printer
There upon the page was the grinning, open armed visage
of a local quasi-celebrity known well as The Preacher
The man had had more Youtube hits
and local access television time than he had sense
As I stared into the color photo at his hollow smile
the hunger pangs returned again
I had never felt so weak
By all that is holy how they did flaunt their ease of existence

# Go To The Gentiles And Preach The Gospel

# Of The Kingdom

# Mary 5:1

Now "Holy Warriors" was a good name for The Preacher
who never wandered far from the pews and ranted of sin
with a book that had never seen a drop of blood
But a few miles away on the front lines of Jerusalem
We were known as "The Thumpers"
We had run the bikers off and at first thought the city ours, but
the heathens had other things in mind
At times I would lie still for days until the sun passed overhead
and spend the night crouched just feet away from my bedroll
with my sights set on one moonlit intersection
with no movement in sight
As I said we did take some in at first when we initially cleared
the streets of Jerusalem
I suppose that's where we got the nickname for our parish's
people, The Thumpers
It's derived from the term "Bible Thumpers"
I suppose some relate the term The Thumpers to our old ways
I suppose some of us relate the term to the blows
the refugees and cowards receive
in the beginning of The Preachers enforced indoctrination
as they surrendered, walking towards us
with bellies to rib cage and blistered hands in the air
I preferred to think of myself as "blessed"
as one of The Thumpers by the impact my rifle butt makes
against my shoulder every time I fire a round
Thump, thump, thump, and down goes another starving man

It wasn't merely bald chagrin that I experienced
every time I killed a sinner
There was also the pleasure I took
in grouping my shots so close to their tattered hearts
The other Thumpers complained for a while
over the conditions they lived in
to keep the relative comfort of the rest of our rather large,
growing parish fed and warm
But as surely as The Preacher received a sign from god
as surely as we began to refer to his tongue as forked
He gave us a new task and we fell upon it
as Goliath before the sling
We fell to it as drunken Noah to a raft
that would fit two of all of the beasts of the world
The word went out as surely as the spite in our mouths
when we heard of our new mission
We were to fall back into more defensible territory
and as the pioneers of this country once had
we were to establish trade and commerce with the people of
this new world
Certain things could not be attained by gunshot and trip wire
Certain things we could not live without
And I
I was to be the one to conduct the trades with the other
warring tribes and scavengers
Perhaps I shouldn't have sent so many complaints back into
The Preacher's ears
Perhaps I shouldn't have questioned
the sins of Eve so long ago
Perhaps I should not have cursed a "goddamn" in his name
when I got the news
but no matter
Perhaps I'll die
Perhaps I'll be lifted to an afterlife of eternal joy and bliss

Perhaps I would do anything
to get off that scorching black, hot tar rooftop
Perhaps I would see my mother again in Hell

# For If You Love Them That Love You

# Jesus 5:46

Her nights could be cold
Best to leave my long leather duster
Her nights could be dangerous
Best to leave my pistol and shotgun
Her nights could be ravenous
Best to tighten my belt and take only what I had of true value
We were down to our last several cans of dog food
We were down to our last candles,
We were down to our last...
I hadn't eaten in two days
Before I slipped out into the night
After waiting for her to succumb to sleep
I stared at the can of Spam and had no shred of hunger
only longing
We had nothing of value to trade
I walked into the night in shoes so worn
they were not worth stealing
I walked into the night a dried husk dangling
from a silk thin strand
Cocooned in desperation
I withered within as I realized that I could not even dare
to touch her one more time before I left
Were I to wake her before leaving unarmed
she would never allow me to venture out
I reflected then, that even gone
I was of more use to her than I was at present
At least then there would be one less stomach

I bolted the door as I left
and walked the streets as a dead man
Refusing to dart from shadow to shadow
Refusing to slink any further
Refusing to die in fear

# The Comforter Will Not Come Unto You;

# But If I Depart, I Will Send Him Unto You

# John 16:7

"I want fresh insulin."
It was all she had to say
I did not sleep the day after she had said those words
I sat with a box in which I had placed every crucifix ever
lifted from a dead man since the hunt had begun so long ago.
There were at least twenty, and most had been stained red
I sat in meditation and prayer
Lowering the sometimes sticky crosses around my head
deliberate and slow, one after another, until the sun set
I carefully spent the day smoothing low all emotion
I pressed down every sentiment of loss, rage, fear, and sorrow
I would venture into my last battle as an iron golem
bent to my very own will
Did I ever mention that....
Before I drowned The Butcher's father, a diabetic man I loved
dearly who had welcomed me into his home unconditionally
Before I had found the true meaning of savage from the
righteous on the streets and in the prison cells after The
Preacher had campaigned to denounce my every breath for
my crime.
Before I sentenced myself to prison in a flash of rage with one
coma-inducing punch to the face of a taunting, foul mouthed,
young man, a member of The Thumpers parish, after a few
too many in a dive bar
Before I ever dropped out of Special Forces on a Section 8
(why didn't they just understand I needed a little more sleep?)

# For Where Thy Treasure Is, There

# Is Thy Heart Also

## Jesus 6:21

I walked into Jerusalem dead ready to end
As I neared the trading post I refused to flinch
The Thumpers had chosen an abandoned gas station
The side streets had been jammed sealed on either side
with husks of cars, barbed wire and fence
The gas station at the end of the street was lit
I could see a fair, blonde girl with gaunt face and ponytail
in blackened fatigues behind the glass
Drumming her fingers unrest across the counter
complete with a late-night drop box
that slides open from the inside
There were two waist high stacks of sandbags
in front of either side of the glass front doors
On the left sat a soot stained man with a deadly shine
machine gun on a tripod with several cans of ammo
On the right stood another man
both in matching filthy fatigues
except this one stood with an AK-47
I knew I appeared true desperate
I slowly walked with confidence to the waiting box
the chisel faced, flint eyed woman opened it as I grew near
"What have you to trade?" she asked forcefully.
I reached into my pocket and withdrew the only thing I had
to prove I owned anything of value and placed it into the
sliding drawer
I said nothing, looking directly at her with conviction

"This is all." I said firmly

# What Binds Me Has Been Slain, And What Turns Me About Has Been Overcome

## Mary 8:21

"We've got one comin in."
said the spotter on the roof on the intercom
"What do you see?" I replied
"He looks desperate, definitely unarmed. Should I take the
shot?" the spotter asked
"Let's see what he has." I replied, "He could be bringing an
offer."
As the man stepped into the light I sneered within
He was Hispanic, dark in skin, eyes, and hair
and thinner than even any of the Thumpers.
He walked slowly, determined yet weak In the chilly night
he wore only a yellowed white undershirt. torn, filthy jeans
and worn shoes
He walked without hesitation
between the stacks of sandbags and armed men
directly to me
"What have you to trade?" I asked, losing my patience
"This is all." he responded with resolve
I pulled the drawer to me after he had emptied his hand
I had expected a list of supply and demand
I had expected a note of verbs and nouns of desperation
I had expected a lot of things
hell even an unavailing green stack of cash
But when I pulled the drawer to me and lifted the contents
into the light
It was not what I had expected

There were two items in the drawer
One was a pregnancy test
It was not foreign to me
I lifted the plastic stick into the light
and saw that the stick showed
a familiar "+" sign
My mouth filled bitter but then I lifted the other item
into the light
It was a polaroid of a tan-skinned woman
With long, black hair, soft features, near gaunt build, and a far
over generous belly, asleep
Lit by candle light
I looked him in his dark eyes wordlessly
"Eight months." was all he said
I looked over my right shoulder into the dark station
packed with supplies
"I need three bed sheets, one tube of diaper cream, a large
container of formula, one baby bottle, some baby aspirin, a
gallon of water, a week of K-rations, and a pack."
I heard myself say
The man behind me switched on a small flashlight
and began to dig through the supplies
"Rip the bed sheets into strips for diapers." I said
He nodded, refusing to smile
I reached for the crucifix around my neck then.
It was a large, wooden, hand carved, lacquer red cross
The carving was a little crude, but it was undeniably a crucifix
The only aspect of Jesus in the crucifix that had any real detail
lay in the rifle I had etched
leaning against his left leg as he dangled from the cross.
I took it from around my neck, grabbed the backpack
and stepped out through the glass doors
I helped the man place the strap around his shoulder
and pressed my crucifix into his palm

"Take this. Find me again…"
He nodded grimly, and I had more kind words to say but…
The intercom squeaked "Incoming"
The headlights from up the street
grew bright and large quite quickly
The machine gun sputtered and the rifles fired and
"Down!" seemed to be the last thing I ever said

# That Whosoever Killeth You Will Think

# That He Doeth God Service

# John 16:2

The last I saw of The Butcher
she was sprinting up a narrow flight of stairs to the rooftop
of a building near the trading post to
look down at our handiwork
She smiled at me, with her bloody, new, razor sharp grin
Rifle and scope bouncing up and down against
the strap over her shoulder
Rifle and scope rubbing against the pack
strapped to her back holding the remote to the SUV
Rifle and scope, pistol and knife, pointed teeth
freshly shaved head, and soot blackened skin

"We don't have to do this you know." I had said before leaving
"What do you want us to do then? Make babies and eat others
until we're the last one's standing." she replied
Then she added
"If we live I think I'll see if I can lose my virginity."
I opened my large, dark hands
and examined the calluses and scars
and as I opened and closed them
rare tears began to fall into my fingers
I caught them in my hands and looked up at her
clenching my damp grip I said,
"You know I've tried to do what I thought was best for us.
To survive."
"It's okay." she said looking up at me fiercely,

"I hate what we have become too."
"It's not your fault." she added,
"I'd be dead now if it weren't for you."
She looked down, oiling her pistol and sliding a part into place
I stood silently trying to compose myself
"I'm more afraid to live than die."
The words fell from her lips
as if she had said them every morning
The words may have well been mine
I nodded, held back more tears
and removed my battered bullet proof vest and helmet
I solemnly let the body armor fall to my side
She stood, shrugged nonchalantly
and wrapped her arms around me
Kissing me on the cheek
"Don't worry. We're not going to die without one another."

I heard faint screams
from the rooftop of the building The Butcher had entered
I saw a body fall, screaming last breath all the way down
and for a moment I believed it to be her
Then the tires of the explosive laden, remote controlled SUV
squealed and tore off down the street toward the trading post
I throttled my motorcycle and followed a block behind
I left the light on my motorcycle off
using the lights of our mobile bomb to see
Ahead was the gas station they had chosen to barter from
It looked like any other station
Shatter proof glass front, shatter proof glass doors, only this
had two stacks of sandbags on either sides of the front
Muzzle flash lit from four points on the station
Two flashes from the roof, a flash behind the bags on the right
and a powerful, lit clatter from the left
I slowed and pulled over in the darkness

The windows of the SUV shattered
The machine gun on the left tore holes
straight through the vehicle
But I had welded steel plates to the radiator and low
over the front tires
It got real close before the machine gun finally hit a tire
The Butcher handled it as beautifully as any final act
She jammed the steering right
just as the front left tire was blown out
And the SUV slid sideways hard, flipping, and tumbling
right into the front of the store
Just as it swept, tumbling and rolling
through the stacks of sandbags and into the building
The Butcher hit the trigger

# All Is Being Dissolved

## Mary 8:17

It was as if a phoenix had given birth in my left eye
I could not tell if my right eye was even still in its socket
But I could feel blood running down the right side of my face
It took a moment to take stock of the rest of me
My left side was pinned under the body of a Thumper and
twisted steel
Beneath me I could feel the bartering man moan and squirm
My right leg was agonizing to move
Only my right arm remained free
It took another moment to realize that the smell
sizzling of fire
Was not my flesh ablaze
The Thumper had been killed by the blast of the tumbling car
And as the car rolled over us
the sandbags had spilled over me
It had protected me from the flames
The fire of the Thumper's burning corpse lying over me began
to gutter a bit
And I could see the burnt husk
that was the front of the building's entrance past his body
The Thumper we had on supply detail in the back of the store
came into view
Orange, yellow, and red flames threw themselves and danced
across him as he slowly died
thrashing and screaming, turning crisp and blackened
I gasped in surprise that I even had breath to draw as
I watched the man die
Just as the living flame hit his knees

a large man came into view
He wore black combat boots and stained, torn jeans and was
bare from the waist up except for
dozens of crucifixes dangling from his neck at his chest
He had streaks and handprints across his chest, arms, and
face in black and red
The only hair upon his head was oiled black and red as well
and stood in one Mohawk strip across his skull
He screamed as he charged at my burning friend and
swung over his head, in a two handed grip, a fireman's axe
He hacked at the burning dead man even long after my friend
had gone corpse still
As he swung his red axe again and again I eased my right arm
slowly to my screaming, broken right leg
I could feel the nine-millimeter still in its holster there
loaded, black and deadly
I drew it slowly and raised my arm to take the shot
I leaned forward slightly to take aim and felt
my mouth begin to fill with red, hot blood
I coughed as my throat went awash and the man turned
taking in the dying woman
pinned under carnage, choking on her own azure, with
one arm free
One arm free and lifted and pointing a loaded pistol at his
chest
I swear he gave the slightest of nods an instant before
I pulled the trigger of the pistol again and again until
he dropped to the scorched ground
Had a prayer even sprung to mind I had not the ability to say it
Black flashed before my eyes as I coughed
blood up from within
Darkness overcame me for a final time
And with it peace

# Deliver Us From Evil

## Jesus 6:13

Darkness came upon me, passed, and came again
When I awoke, gasping beneath
a pile of bodies, sandbags, and charred steel
For a moment I questioned who and where I was
For a moment after, I questioned whether or not
I was still alive
For a moment after that, I questioned how
I filled my lungs with air several times and began to squirm
The dawn was breathing across the edge of the night sky
I dragged myself free then, weak, bloody sore and exhausted
The front of the store had been blasted open malefactory
Smoke still rose thick curls from body and building
It was so quiet I could hear birds chirping
I grabbed the barrel of a blackened AK-47 and used it to pry
the mostly intact bag I had received free from the wreckage
The woman who had thrown me down before the explosion
Past salvage
Past saving
Past my hands
I took a moment to say a blessing over her
Closing her one open eye with a prayer
Then I began to limp home
It seemed like an agonizing hour dragging
twisted leg to make several blocks
When I looked over my shoulder I saw that I was leaving a
slowly leaking trail of baby formula in
my wake from the torn pack
I set the bag down and numbly rearranged it

By the time I had made it nearly home the sun was half up
behind me
The day was a deadly time to be in plain sight
I limped ragged bloody on
Relief flowing through me and putting strength to my every
pain wracked movement

It took a moment to register the sound
A low roar that had not been heard in so long it was alien

I turned, dropping the bag of supplies
weakly off my shoulder in the process, and looked up
It was a plane
Flying in low
The lights in the wings were flashing
I stood gawking into the air as something fell from the plane
It dropped slowly, landing close to my very door
I ran my dry tongue across my blistered lips and dragged
my bag behind me to the green, canvass package
complete with parachute blowing in the wind
I leaned down and ran my hand across the canvass fabric
It read "U.S. Army"
I laughed
I had not laughed in so long
Grinning so broadly it split the skin in my chapped lips I gave
the signature knock at the steel door of my home
She emerged to pull the package within our home with my
help
And as I trimmed the strings of the parachute she gazed into
the sunrise and wept
She hadn't left the house in nine months
We dragged the package inside and we opened it
And the cans of food and supplies spilled out
onto our kitchen floor

We held each other and moaned with relief then
Her swollen belly pressing into me
God Bless
We were going to be okay

# Bring No More Vain Oblations...

## It Is Iniquity

## Isaiah 1:13

I emerged from my interpretation of a tortured mortal's thoughts, hope, dreams and soul itself into a form I was unfamiliar with.

I found myself stirred into being by the mists of existence into a scene I was entirely unprepared for.

The carpeting was a thick white shag. The couch against the wall of the small room was a large, crush red, plush, expensive piece. The coffee table placed before the couch was of dark wood polished gleaming and carved: topped with an innate crystalline bowl filled with to overflowing with fruit glistening with dew.

The dressing room was small and dominated on one side by a mirror that stretched across its length and a makeup counter below it.

I had been merging and swelling from my consciousness, to others, to the afterlife for so long I was disorientated for a moment.

The counter was the first thing that came into awareness. It had several bottles of what looked like perfume and make-up. Placed before me upon the counter were two large, ring-bearing hands. They were brown as I was accustomed, but manicured and flawless, as I was not accustomed. They were mine.

Proportion was understandably a little hard to establish, having just been born into a new dimension, as you may or may not be able to imagine. In the mirror before me was a new form.

My jawline was stronger. My features more striking. It was and was not my countenance. I was larger across the shoulders, in physique, and height. I was dressed into a tailored tuxedo and my new body curved with the implications of a form only many years in the gym and blessed genetics could ever create.

Now all this is rather hard to describe and perhaps a bit even less comprehensible than anything thus presented to you. It was recognizable enough to keep me from becoming too alarmed.

I was an angel.

There were the wings.

I could feel the bones jutting from my shoulder blades. At their peak they rose above the top of my head. The tips of them brushed slightly against the shag carpeting, and when I stretched them to their span and fluttered them a bit with muscles I had never felt the use of, well, let's just say I had never felt so beautiful or powerful in my conscious existence.

The wings were composed of long, white, soft feathers, and had a rainbow sheen to them. A sheen a bit like the one seen in a layer of oil in the sunlight of a mud puddle. Every movement glimmered with colors.

I fluttered them a bit then, and felt the lift even a small movement brought about.

After I stretched them a bit and after glancing around at the room I took a few steps from the mirror. I stood to my new seemingly considerable height, flexed my muscles and wrapped the wings slightly around myself smiling into the mirror.

"I have to admit. I am one beautiful being." I said aloud at my reflection, grinning with a perfectly aligned, white set of teeth.

A bright light filled the room then. I squinted my eyes and looked into the doorway that had appeared and there was a shadow of a large figure.

"You're on, sir."

The voice was deep and as I shielded my eyes and approached the doorway I made out the backlit figure before me.

It was hunched over in the doorway. Two large, black horns stretched from either side of its head. It had a great muzzle, protruding tusks, and at the end of a large bull's head there was a golden nose ring. His height loomed.

He was a minotaur.

He wore a short sleeved black t-shirt and black slacks, was covered in combed, thick black hair, and held a clipboard in one large hand and a stack of notecards in the other. He had an intercom complete with an earplug and an mouthpiece fitted nicely to the head of a bull.

"Come with me sir. You're on. We have a speech prepared." He said handing me a stack of blue stationery.

He then snorted slightly, grinning to expose large, slightly yellowing molars and said, "Welcome to the 133rd tier of Heaven, sir."

"I won't need the speech my friend. I think I know just what to say."

The minotaur's tail flicked about and he politely but quickly led me through several long, narrow hallways as his earpiece squawked incessantly so loudly even I could hear it.

The next thing I knew I was being led from behind a curtain onto a small stage. There was a podium at the center. On the other side of the stage behind the curtain I could see a cherub holding a microphone announcing my arrival. He looked to be an oversized, fat, white baby with a small set of wings in a tuxedo. He was rosy cheeked and dimpled and he flashed a great false smile at me as I was pressed onto the stage. I could only make out the last of what he had said as I was led on from the crackling sound system, but it ended with, "Welcome the youngest soul to ever reach the 133rd tier of heaven, Isaiah Freeman."

I looked out into the room. It was a small ballroom of attractive people, apparently human, in tuxedos and ballroom gowns sitting at tables complete with candles and mostly empty plates.

I walked to the podium with a microphone and glared out at them. Just off to the front was a teleprompter manned by another well dressed cherub standing upon a stool. He "Ahem'd" loudly and motioned to the words as they crossed the screen of the device.

The room was as if I was accepting an award in any hotel ballroom in any city.

I looked blankly at the faces. I looked judgingly at the prompter. The words "I'd like to thank God first and foremost, and thank you for having me." Began to cross the screen.

I'd had enough.

I began, "This entire ordeal has been an affront to any thoughtful decent beings concept of humanity. I don't know of what almighty consciousness created all this mess. Given what I have experienced, I would have to say they should not remain unmedicated. There is no chemical or psychological justification for the suffering I have witnessed before and after my death for nearly any living being of Earth."

I gave the crowd a real good pause then. Nothing like a real good dramatic pause. As I glared at them I saw their stiff faces and uncomfortable composure. In this crowd I saw little comprehension of what I was trying to get across.

I grew short tempered. I began to yell.

"Can anyone tell me why there are no brown people in this audience! I may submit a request to entry into hell!"

I found myself gritting my teeth in anger, and once again giving them a real good beat of tense silence, but I heard laughter from the back left. I was wrong. There was one brown skinned being in the cheap seats, and he was laughing his ass off at an otherwise uncomfortable table of three. My eyes widened but the handsome tuxedoed man merely rose from his feet, gave me a firm thumbs up, and yelled "Do you have any idea how long the wait list is to get into hell?"

I continued, "I suffered through every moment in John's jail sentence. I felt the loss of The Baptist as he prepared himself and the only one he loved to die!"

"Our creator made Mary self righteous! Our creator taught her to kill through the circumstances of the existence he gave her! Every night she lay awake wracked in tears is carved into me!" I said.

"You would give me accolade for watching Jesus starve to spare his pregnant wife the last cans of dog food! You would give me the power to surpass time, space, and consciousness only to leave me without the means to ensure his child survived!" At this point I was spitting the words more than saying them.

The cherub approached from stage right now, holding his microphone and motioning to the monstrous hairy stagehands. The minotaurs approached from behind the curtains. Their size and flaring nostrils were less than encouraging.

Then it occurred to me.

"Eva! Eva! Do any of you even know or care of her! The Butcher! What happened to the young woman known as The Butcher! Do any of you even care of the fate of a child forced to endure horror as you sit glaring at me in tuxedos?" I yelled.

Large hairy beasts with bloodshot eyes and horned heads towering over my own rushed from either side of the stage to drag me away.

My newfound form was no match for them, but I was not going to go down easy. I threw my good elbow, a left, straight into the jaw of one of the monstrous creations as they grappled with me.

It felt as if I had just slammed my arm into a titanium cinderblock.

The beast did not even flinch. He pulled one massive fist back as he snorted hard into my face, and then, my fair fellow creatures of God, I felt as if a titanium cinderblock had just slammed into my right eye. Never underestimate the strength and the size of fist of a minotaur.

I had last words, but they came out all garbled alphabet soup, and as I crumpled to the floor, the darkness came upon me.

Then.... Well then my horrified audience members, I felt my consciousness slip and wrap itself into the one of a young woman with a head-splitting pain.

# And God Divided The Light From The Darkness

## Genesis 1:4

I awoke flat on my back with a ringing in my head
the equal of a pulsing thunderclap
I gingerly raised my hand to my face, when I returned it
to my eyes it was red at the fingertips
After probing the wound at my temple it appeared that the
sniper's bullet had grazed the side of my head
It had just missed my skull
It was a miracle
I realized soon after, curled in the fetal position in pain
followed by grief
John The Baptist was dead
Had he any strength he would have come for me by now
The sun was setting in the west and I clenched my drumbeat
throb of a head and gazed out over Jerusalem
The smoke from the explosion still rose from the trading post
I looked west into the setting sun down the distant highway
I could just make out in my scope Humvees in the distance
making their way through miles of abandoned vehicle
I guess the rest of the world existed after all
I guess the end is not always final
I guess I may have to live
I took a travel bottle of aspirin, a bottle of water
and a bag of jerky from my pack
I settled in
Best to let them find me

Best to play the victim
Best to fit myself back into the jigsaw puzzle
of the world that remained
As a child I had always wanted to be a chef
As a fifteen-year old girl I had wanted to be a surgeon
I had not expected God to give me another try
The Butcher had been killed with a fatal miss last night
I cannot say for certain, but I may not miss her
I began to pray